RESOURCE BANK

SPELLING

CONTENTS

INTRODUCTION   1

SPELLING STRATEGIES   4

SPELLING AND GRAMMAR   10

HISTORY AND INFLUENCES   24

About this book

In the early stages of learning to spell, many children rely upon the sounds they can hear and their knowledge, however incomplete, of how those sounds are represented using the letters of the alphabet. A programme of learning to hear, read and write the 40+ phonemes (speech sounds) of English will enable children to spell phonemically by the end of Key Stage 1/P3–4. As children move towards more conventional spelling, they need to rely less on sounding out words and more on visual memory. Unfortunately for many children, the complexities of the spelling system often prove overwhelming for their visual memory and this, in turn, tends to limit the effectiveness of Look–Read–Cover–Write–Check as the sole method of teaching spelling.

It is for this reason that children need to be guided through the maze of spelling so that they discover and learn some of the patterns and guidelines that will be useful to them when visual memory fails. The activities in this book and the accompanying poster will help you act as their guide. There is still a place for training the visual memory through Look–Read–Cover–Write–Check. This need not be at odds with an investigative approach, as encouraged and described in this book, which involves children in the collection of data and a consideration of any patterns thrown up by it. They can then come to some conclusions and understanding of how the system works. If this can be linked to an explanation of how the system came to be, then there is a greater chance of them internalising the learning.

PRVNTia

INTRODUCTION

This book is divided into three sections:

◆ Spelling strategies – this looks at ways of accelerating and consolidating early spelling skills, together with ideas on developing independent spelling strategies of the kind outlined in the 'spelling strategies' section of the 'Word Level work' of the National Literacy Strategy's *Framework for Teaching*.

◆ Spelling and grammar – this looks at the way in which grammar and meaning are reflected in spelling.

◆ History and influences – this covers the evolution of the English spelling system and the 'stories' behind some words which will help to explain their spellings.

About developing spelling skills in Key Stage 2/P4–7

There are broadly three principles governing the way the English spelling system works.

The first is that the way in which sounds are written is dependent on context. For example, the letters 'ck' are used to represent /k/ at the end of CVC (consonant-vowel-consonant) words with a short vowel, but the letter 'k' is used after long vowels – compare lack/lake. Photocopiable pages 7 and 8 show the consonant sounds and the major different ways in which they are written. Where context influences spelling, this is clearly indicated.

Second, grammar, meaning and spelling are closely linked. Words are made of building blocks or 'morphemes'. There are two types of morpheme – 'free' ones as in bookcase in which both parts of the word can stand alone (book + case), and 'bound' ones as in boy**s**, **de**scribe and happi**ness**, in which the morphemes -**s**, **de-** and -**ness** are not meaningful on their own. Furthermore, bound morphemes can come before or after the root form (boy, scribe and happy, in these examples) of words. They are called 'affixes'. Those that come before the root are called 'prefixes' and those that come after are called 'suffixes'. Prefixes allow new words to be built out of root words – describe, inscribe, prescribe. Suffixes can be used to change the meaning of the root word – that is to say, in a derivational way – friend to friend**ship**, free to free**dom**. They can also be used in an inflectional way – I jump**ed**; they**'re**. (These are all covered in the objectives of the NLS *Framework*.)

Finally, it is a fact that when words are imported into English, they retain all or some of their original spelling. This accounts for the often conflicting information the eyes and ears receive when learning to spell. For example, the words teach**er**, calend**ar**, doct**or** and gymkhan**a** all have the same final sound, but there are four different spellings. The 'er' of 'teacher' is the more usual way of representing this sound. The other three were all imported at some time: 'calendar' from Latin 'Kalendae'; 'doctor' from Latin 'docere' and 'gymkhana' from Hindi. The words in our language reflect our history and as such can be a rich source of interest to children. They need to understand that as the English language expanded and evolved, attempts were made to orchestrate the development of the spelling system. It was not until 1755 with the publication of Johnson's *A Dictionary of the English Language* that there was an authority for stabilizing this development.

About investigating spelling

Spelling, however, is not static and there continues to be development today, particularly with the influence of advertising. For this reason, we need to present spelling to children as a dynamic, living force in our lives.

To nurture this interest you have the poster in this book. You will also need dictionaries that show the origins of words. Ruth Brown's children's book *A Four-tongued Alphabet* (Red Fox) is an excellent introduction to the relationship between English and other European languages. Photocopiable page 9 provides a format for investigating spelling. It is desirable but not vital to start investigations through the use of a shared text; this allows you to introduce the spelling feature to be examined in an uncontrived way. You could use food packaging/ labels/advertisements to initiate or support investigations, as well as the shared text, other books in the classroom and the children's spelling in their own work. Investigations work well when carried out as group activities, with the children working in pairs within the group and coming together to pool their data (the words found) and their observations at the end. Photocopiable page 9 can be used in either A3 or A4 format for recording purposes. At this stage, you might want to encourage the children to think of a reason for the patterns that have been observed. When each group has had a chance to investigate and draw conclusions (which may be right or wrong, as in all scientific investigations), you can record together the class's observations on an A3 version of page 9. At this point, it would be appropriate to discuss the findings, drawing on the children's own conclusions, and use the poster to clarify, extend, validate or challenge the children's thinking. This is illustrated below.

This is what we have to investigate.
words with 'gh' in them

This is the list we made.
enough fight straight height weight rough ghost plough high weigh ghastly laugh

This is what we noticed.
'gh' comes at the beginning, in the middle and at the end of words. At the end it can be silent or make a 'f' sound.

This is what we found out.
We looked at the poster and found out that printers from Holland liked the letters 'gh' together... and... and...

We are going to check this by collecting more examples.
We are going to check the different sounds made by 'gh' in different places in words by collecting more examples.

Preparing to use the poster

Many of the activities are directly related to the objectives of the NLS *Framework*. The A1 poster that accompanies this book is designed to support the activities. The black and white side covers the evolution of the English spelling system – as seen through the eyes of a cow. (The word 'alphabet' comes to us via Greek from the Phoenician 'aleph' meaning 'ox' and 'beth' meaning 'shed', hence the choice of a cow as guide.) You can enlarge the A4 sections to A3 to share and bind together as a big book or frieze to use with the children. Alternatively, you can make A4 booklets. Either format can be used as a vehicle for familiarizing children with the history of our language. This information will form the backdrop to the study of spelling and the associated activities and, therefore, you need to work through the poster and acquaint the children with the broad outline of the evolution of English. A detailed examination of each section can take place at an appropriate point; for example, when studying 'gh' at the beginnings or endings of words, you could look at section 6 of the black and white poster and refer to William Caxton and the Dutch printers.

The coloured side of the poster provides additional teaching resources: an introduction to the major prefixes and suffixes of English and their derivations.

LET'S LOOK AT THE POSTER

GROUP SIZE AND ORGANIZATION
Whole class
DURATION
20 minutes
LEARNING OBJECTIVE
To become familiar with the poster and begin to follow the story of the English language.

YOU WILL NEED
The black and white side of the poster 'The history of English', large sheets of paper, marker pens.

WHAT TO DO
Familiarize the children with the layout and stories on the black and white side of the poster 'The history of English'. You will return many times to this poster. Ask:
◆ *Which historical times are shown?* (1. Celts and Brythons 2. Roman invasion 3. Anglo-Saxon invasion 4. More Anglo-Saxons – the Augustinian and Benedictine monks 5. Norman monks 6. 15th century Dutch printers 7. 16th century scholars 8. 18th–20th centuries.)
◆ *Do you know anything else about these times/people?* For example, you may be studying invaders or Tudors or Britain since 1930, and can focus on the part of the poster showing changes to our language that occurred during the period being studied.

An excellent starting point is to give groups of children nonsense words to spell. Hand out large sheets of paper and marker pens so that they are encouraged to write collaboratively in large script. Compare the versions of the nonsense words devised by the different groups and encourage children to put forward a case for their version. Liken this to the debate that went on in history among scholars. Capture their interest and allow them to investigate!

SPELLING STRATEGIES

CONSOLIDATION OF EARLY SKILLS

In order for children to have a firm basis on which to build an understanding of the spelling system, it is essential that they can identify the sounds in words and represent them correctly in the most common spellings. You may find it is necessary to do some work to consolidate the children's learning from KS1/P1–3.

The strategies in this section will help you to secure the KS1/P1–3 work. For example, when faced with having to write 'weight', a Year 3 child may write 'wait' which should be accepted as plausible, although you should point out the conventional spelling with an explanation. If children write 'wayt', then the teaching here should involve helping children to understand that 'ay' is used finally in words like 'play'. Some children will need time to consolidate their learning of this basic system and to refine their understanding of it. The NLS *Framework* refers to the need to 'secure phonemic spellings from previous terms' and to 'consolidate the spelling of words containing each of the long vowel phonemes from KS1'. It is significant that the vowel phonemes cause the biggest problems and, for this reason, the activities outlined on pages 5–6 concentrate on them, although they could be adapted to cover consonant phonemes. (Where appropriate, the activities in this book include Year and Term references to the NLS *Framework*: Year 5 Term 2 = Y5/2. The Scottish Primary equivalents are shown as P6, for example.)

Find out which parts of the system children need to consolidate. You can do this by analyzing children's written work (or by asking children to spell the words from List 3 in the NLS *Framework*.) You can then prepare bingo cards based on the phonemes to be learned – see below:

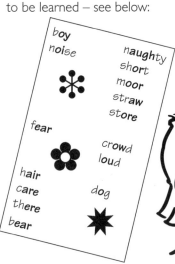

Play this game two or three times a week in small groups. Follow up by asking the children questions such as those shown below:

◆ *How many different ways are there of writing 'oy'?*
◆ *Which one is used at the beginning or in the middle of words?*
◆ *How do you think you might spell 'ointment'? Will it be 'oi' or 'oy'? Let's see which group can find it first in the dictionary.*

Alternatively, provide the children with five consonant skeletons (a word in which the letters responsible for the vowels have been omitted) and cards with the five vowel phonemes written on them. The object is to make words by matching the appropriate phonemes to the skeletons. See which group can complete their skeleton first. Let them use a dictionary to check their spelling.

Another game is to write words on the flip chart or board and, with children working in teams, get them to come up and rub out the letters responsible for vowel phonemes.

A version of 'Simon says' can be played with a magic slate or words written in magnetic letters:

SPELLING STRATEGIES

A final game would be to play 'snap' or 'pairs' using a pack of cards with words on representing the range of vowel sounds (see the illustration below). The children have to link the cards based on the phonemes they contain. For example: pie, bite, peach, tree, and so on.

| pie | bite | peach | tree |

ASSESSMENT

It is very important to assess the children's growing understanding of the spelling system. This can be done through analyzing their work (or by giving the words in List 3 again) after four weeks of these games. It will also help if you share the goal of the activities in terms of a target as shown below:

We are learning to write the vowel sounds of English.		
Names	Week 1	Week 2
Samina	This week I have learnt…	
Matt	This week I have learnt…	

IDEAS FOR DISPLAY

It is worth considering dedicating display space to the study of spelling. Each week, you can reflect with the class on their learning and record it. It provides an area for keeping current investigations and highlights the importance you attach to spelling.

IDEAS FOR DIFFERENTIATION

When investigating spelling, the children should be working at their own level and differentiation should not be a significant issue. Therefore, there are few additional differentiation suggestions offered for the activities in this book. The NLS *Framework*, for example, allows for children to work in the word level strand at the Year appropriate to their current knowledge rather than according to their age. For example, a Year 5 child might be doing Year 3 word-level work. Every effort would, of course, be needed in order to fast track such a child to the part of the *Framework* that matches their chronological age.

The following activities all begin with whole-class work, followed by reinforcement through individual work. The whole-class teaching is intended to take about 15 minutes; ongoing time should then be allocated for the children's individual work.

WOBBLY SPELLING

LEARNING OBJECTIVE
To identify words they are unsure of how to spell.

YOU WILL NEED
A copy of *Winnie-The-Pooh* by A.A. Milne (Methuen).

WHAT TO DO
Read the class the story 'Eeyore has a birthday' from *Winnie-The-Pooh*. In this Pooh Bear talks about his spelling being 'good spelling but it Wobbles'. This is a supportive starting point. As the children write, encourage them to draw a wobbly line under spellings of which they are unsure. The children can then go back and examine these spellings at the end of the piece of work. In this way, the flow of writing is not interrupted and children gain a sense of satisfaction working independently in this way.

Children can be trained to move from 'wobbly' to 'good' spelling through watching you model the skill in shared writing: *Does this spelling look right?* Encourage them to look carefully at their spellings and check:
◆ the order of the letters
'Belwo! Have I got the letters right for the vowel sound? I know that vowel letters come first when you write vowel sounds, so, no... I have not!'
◆ the context
'Magic!' I know that in words that have two syllables and end in 'ic' it has to be 'i' and 'c', NOT 'i-c-k', so that's OK.
◆ the length of the word
I know that 'catastrophe' is a long word. It's one of those words you can easily miss bits off, like 'conservatory'. It doesn't look long enough. Have I got all the syllables?
◆ if their 'wobbly' spelled word rhymes with a word they know how to spell
'Bright'. Mmmm... I know, it's like 'light'!
◆ Alternatively, it may be a word that is related to another word they know
Sign. I know it's like 'signal' so it must have a 'g' in it.

ASSESSMENT
Assess children's range of spelling strategies by asking them what they would do, or ask for 'advice' from them in shared writing.

SPELLING STRATEGIES

HOW TO USE A DICTIONARY

LEARNING OBJECTIVE
To become familiar with the application of alphabetical order in a dictionary.

YOU WILL NEED
Class dictionaries, word cards representing one page of the dictionary (see below), photocopiable pages 7–8 enlarged for shared reading, paper or card strips (about 15cm × 9cm), marker pen.

WHAT TO DO
Children need to understand how to use a dictionary. Most KS2/P4–7 children cope with alphabetical order, though some find it hard to understand how alphabetical order dictates the order of words under any given letter.

A useful starting point is to take words from a page in a dictionary, write them on to individual cards and lay them out one under the other in a haphazard fashion. Ask the children to find particular words from the jumbled ones. Discuss how difficult it is to do this quickly. Compare this to a situation in which a postman has to deliver letters to addresses in a street in which the house numbers are in the wrong order. The numbers might all begin with the digit '1' but the units are mixed up. Talk about the same thing happening with words if we order them just according to their initial letter. Using the dictionary page from which you have taken the words, ask the children to suggest a solution to the problem. Steer the discussion so that alphabetical order is identified as the guiding principle.

You could also look at the dictionary page together and explain how the information is presented, for example the different fonts, abbreviations, definitions, derivations, and so on.

Children also need to know that some sounds are going to cause them problems. Use the charts on photocopiable pages 7 and 8 to highlight these. For example, /f/ can be represented by the letters 'f' and 'ph'. Alert the children to this and use the opportunity for them to explore which way of writing /f/ is more common by counting the words or pages devoted to 'f' in the dictionary as opposed to 'ph'. (This is where you could start looking in detail at the languages that have contributed to making English, using the black and white poster and/or Ruth Brown's book – see Introduction, page 2.)

Finally, during shared writing, model how to tackle polysyllabic words. Have a supply of strips of paper or card. When you want to write a polysyllabic word, show the children how to clap out the syllables first. (Sometimes the way we say words obscures the number of syllables, for example, dictionary = 'dic-shun-ry'. Don't worry about that at this stage). Draw a box on the strip of paper or card with compartments on it to correspond to the number of syllables identified. With the children's help, have a go at spelling each syllable in turn. Then use the strip to help you scan for the word in the dictionary. Write the conventional spelling above the syllables. Compare and contrast the two versions.

IDEAS FOR DISPLAY
Display the two versions of your polysyllabic spellings with a note of what has been learned:

We have learned that the 'shun' sound in dictionary is written using 'tion' and that sometimes when we say words we miss bits we should write.

d i c t i o n a r y

| dic | shun | ry |

IDEAS FOR DIFFERENTIATION
As children find their way with your help through the spelling maze, they may need a support mechanism such as a 'writing mat'. This is a piece of laminated A4 paper or card on which either you or the child can write any points that may temporarily be causing problems. If you use a non-permanent OHP pen, you can easily remove the examples so that the mat can be re-used by the same or another child.

The farmers <u>said</u> that they had <u>paid</u> all their money for the goose that <u>laid</u> the golden egg.

SPELLING STRATEGIES

Name _____   Date _____

Consonant sounds (1)

p	penguin
-pp	apple

b	butter
bb-	bubble (following short vowel)
Bh	Bhatti (Hindi)

k	kettle, kitten
kh	khaki (Urdu)
c	cat, cot, cut
-cc-	accord (prefix)
-ck	lack (following short vowel)
ch	character (Greek)

g	goat
-gg-	bigger (following short vowel)
-gg-	aggressive (prefix)
gh	ghost (from the Dutch)
gu	guard (French)

NB k does team with a, o and u, but these words are often unusual.

t	tortoise
-tt-	letter (following short vowel)
Th	Thames
pt	pterodactyl (Greek)

d	dog
-dd-	adder (following short vowel)
-dd-	address (prefix)
Dh	Dhillon (Hindi)

m	man
-mm-	summer (following short vowel)
-mm-	committee (prefix)
mb	climb (lost its sound)
mn	column (lost its sound)

n	net
-nn-	dinner (following short vowel)
-nn-	announce (prefix)
gn	gnaw (Old English)
-gn	sign (lost its sound)
kn	knee (German)
pn	pneumatic (Greek)

PHOTOCOPIABLE
RESOURCE
BANK

SPELLING STRATEGIES

Name _____   Date _____

Consonant sounds (2)

f	fish
-ff	cuff (following short vowel)
ph	photograph (Greek)
-gh	enough (Dutch printers)

j	jam
ge	gem (Latin)
gi	giant (Latin)
gy	gyrate (Latin)
-ge	page (following long vowel)
-dge	badge (following short vowel)
-gg-	suggest (prefix)

sh	ship
ch	chef (French)
-si-	mansion (Latin)
-ti-	nation (Latin)
-ci-	precious, special (Latin)
-sci-	conscious (Latin)
-ce-	ocean (Greek)

-s-	measure (Latin)
-z-	seizure (French)
-ge	beige

s	sun
ss	dress (following short vowel)
-ss-	assert (prefix)
c + e, i or y	centre, city (Latin)
sc + e, i or y	scene, scythe, science
ps-	psychology (Greek)

r	rabbit
-rr-	furry (short vowel)
-rr-	surreptitious (prefix)
wr	write (German)
rh	rhododendron (Greek)

l	lorry
-ll	bell (short vowel final position)
ll-	yellow (following short vowel)
ll-	llama (Spanish)
-l	deal (long vowel final position)

ch-	cheese
-tch	match (final position)
-ture	picture (Latin)
-tion	question (Latin)

Name _____   Date _____

Investigating spelling

This is what we have to investigate.

This is the list we made.

This is what we noticed.

This is what we found out.

We are going to check this by collecting more examples.

SPELLING AND GRAMMAR

book/case

The activities in this section are all designed to start from a stimulus word. This can come from a shared text and can be used with the whole class or with a small group. The introduction should take about 15 minutes and the follow-up work should take 20 minutes. Often the study can continue on a more informal basis after the initial focus, with further examples being added to the class or individual collection. It is worth considering providing each child with a 'Spelling study book', in which he or she can record spelling investigations and learning, collect examples of new words, devise games/posters/spelling quiz questions and so on.

The NLS *Framework* Year and Term references are given in brackets at the end of the learning objectives.

SUFFIXES FOR PLURALITY

LEARNING OBJECTIVES
To learn about the concept of plurality and begin to explore how the language indicates this through the use of 's' and 'es'. (Y3/2; P4)

YOU WILL NEED
The coloured side of the poster, a shared text with examples of the words to be studied, highlighter pens, board or flip chart, make an enlarged copy of photocopiable page 9 (investigation sheet) for class/group investigation.

WHAT TO DO

LESSON ONE

Introduction: Introduce the concept of plurality with the children by drawing a blobby monster on the board and labelling it as shown:
Explain that this 'zug' is all alone. He is single. Then draw a plus sign and another zug:
First we had one zug. Now we have two...
(pause for the children to say 'zugs').

ONE ZUG

The previous section looked largely at the smallest units for making words – phonemes – and strategies to consolidate children's early word-building skills. This section looks at another set of word-building blocks – morphemes. More information about these can be found in the Introduction on page 2, as well as in this section up to and including the activity 'Compound words' on page 16.

In addition, homophones (to, two, too) are dealt with in this section as their use is determined by their grammatical function.

The coloured side of the poster illustrates (at the top) the changes prefixes and suffixes can bring about to words. Use the poster and a shared text with the feature you wish to study to support the activities outlined on the following pages. Spaces have been left on the poster so that labels can be attached to denote parts of speech. These have been left blank deliberately for the children to add labels themselves using pieces of card and Blu-Tack, following discussion and the appropriate activity.

SPELLING AND GRAMMAR

Draw attention to the plus sign. Ask the children whether they have seen it before and what it means. Introduce the word 'plus' as an alternative to 'add'. Point to the first 'zug', remind the children that he is single and say that words like this are called 'singular'. Now introduce the word 'plural' in relation to plus: *First we had one zug, singular. Now we have one zug plus another one, we have two or plural.* Write the words down so that children can see the connections.

Now refer to the shared text and with the children's help, highlight words that are plural. (At this point, do not give them the word 'noun'. Children will discover this for themselves later.) Ask the children what they notice about the words they have underlined. They will almost certainly observe that the words end in 's'.

Independent work: set up an investigation (see Introduction, pages 2–3) whereby the children collect words that are plural.

Plenary: Using your enlarged copy of photocopiable page 9, record the children's 'plural' words and what they have learned. You will find that the children have collected a lot of words that are plural and that all the words will have 's' on the end, but not all the 's' ending words will be plural. Use this opportunity to move the children's learning on by drawing attention to the fact that some words are the names of things (nouns), whereas others are not proper (or singular) words when the 's' is taken away. Discuss this and record your conclusions on the photocopiable sheet:

◆ *What do you notice about these words – woods, cats, pages, pencils, princesses? Are they the names of things or do they tell us what someone did?*

◆ *What happens if I take the 's' away from this word: THIS. Is it still a word?*

◆ *So what kinds of words can be made into plural?*

At the end of this lesson you should have established that plurals pertain to nouns. The aim of the next lesson is to examine in more detail how the language indicates plurality through spelling. At this point it would be appropriate to draw attention to the part of the poster which explains that suffixes can change nouns and to look at the words it gives as examples.

Introduction: many nouns form the plural by adding 's'. Some have to add 'es' to make saying them easier. Try saying 'snishs' for example.

Revise the previous lesson by returning to the poster and discussing what you learned together. Now write some nonsense words and draw some accompanying pictures on the board and ask the children to make them plural: bip, flub, snish, slose, dax, murch: *This is a bip.* (Point to the picture of a 'bip'.) *Bip is the name of this creature. The word 'bip' is a noun. Can you make this word plural?* (Pause for the answer.) *How would we write it?* (Invite children to come up and have a go.)

Repeat with the other words. Write 's' and 'es', the suffixes (morphemes) that mark plurality, in a different colour. Ask the children what they notice. Explore why the last four (snish, slose, dax and murch) have to take /iz/ ('es'). Refer again to the poster and to the words the children collected in the previous lesson.

Independent work: encourage the children to have a go at making up nonsense nouns, illustrating them and writing them in the plural. Tell them that they must include nouns that end in 's' and 'es'. These can then be displayed.

Plenary: draw the activity together by referring to the learning of the lesson in relation to the nonsense words the children have made, their use of 's' or 'es' and the reasons for their choices.

EXTENSION WORK

Keep the investigation open by displaying the enlarged photocopiable sheet or keeping it in an 'investigation' book with a list of ongoing investigations on the display board. Collect words that do not follow the pattern, for example, foot – feet, child – children, piano – pianos, tomato – tomatoes (see page 27, 'Vowels at the end of words' for more on end vowels other than 'e'), fly – flies, donkey – donkeys, loaf – loaves. These and related words can then become the focus of separate investigations and speculation in themselves.

SPELLING AND GRAMMAR

MARKING TIME

LEARNING OBJECTIVES
To learn about the concept of tense and start to explore how the language indicates this through spelling. (Y4/1; P5)

YOU WILL NEED
A remote control handset, shared text with examples of verbs in the past tense, an enlarged copy of photocopiable page 9, marker pens.

WHAT TO DO
NB This activity deals with the past tense. It is possible to adapt this approach to cover the present tense marker '-s' and the present participle marker 'ing'. There are rules governing their use. For example, where verbs end in '-y', the 'y' is changed to 'i' before 'es' is added. (Note the similarity with plurals.) Where the verb ends in 'e', it is taken away before adding 'ing', (Note that the suffixes 'ed' and 'ing' reappear in the activity, 'Doubling consonants' on page 28.)

Introduction: introduce the concept of tense as follows:

◆ *Which button on the video machine do you press if you want to watch the film?* (Play)
◆ *Which button do you press if you want to watch something that has already happened?* (Rew)
◆ *Which button do you press if you want to skip a bit of the film and watch something that is coming up?* (Ffw)

Go through the shared text and highlight verbs in the past tense. Enter these onto your enlarged copy of photocopiable page 9. As you do so, say them aloud and discuss the different sounds you can hear at the end, for example jumped = /t/, wagged = /d/, wanted = /id/.

Independent work: set the children the task of sorting the verbs according to how the endings sound. They can use photocopiable page 9 for this. Get them to think of, or find, more that fit the three patterns. Is 'ed' always used at the end?

Plenary: record the children's findings on your enlarged copy of photocopiable page 9. Draw them together and conclude, with reference to the poster, that 'ed' is a suffix that indicates the past tense and that it can have three sounds.

EXTENSION WORK
Continue collecting past tense verbs. If the children find any verbs that do not make their past tense with 'ed', follow up with the activity 'Irregular verbs' below.

Get the children to make up their own verbs and then illustrate them. Their verbs should end in 'ed' and use all three pronunciations.

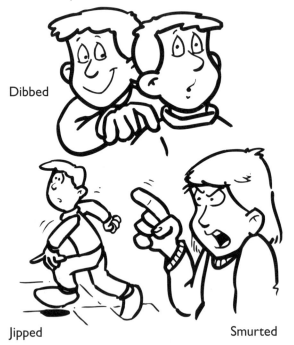

Dibbed

Jipped   Smurted

IRREGULAR VERBS

LEARNING OBJECTIVES
To explore and learn about irregular ways of making past tense forms. (Y4/1; P5)

YOU WILL NEED
A shared text with examples of irregular verbs, different coloured highlighter pens, enlarged copies of photocopiable pages 9 and 18, a selection of books on medieval life such as *The Luttrell Village* by Sheila Sancha (Collins), writing materials.

SPELLING AND GRAMMAR

WHAT TO DO

This activity should follow the work on verbs that form the past tense using the suffix 'ed' (see 'Marking time' on page 12). Verbs that form their past tense through other means are irregular and are called 'strong verbs'. These verbs generally describe everyday activities in people's lives centuries ago. They describe the weather, agricultural activities, human transactions, and so on.

LESSON ONE

Introduction: recap the concept of past tense with the children, then go through your shared text underlining the verbs in the past tense with a highlighter pen. Discuss the past tense marker 'ed' and its various pronunciations. Ask if all the verbs end in 'ed'. Highlight in a different colour those which do not. Enter them onto your enlarged copy of photocopiable page 9.

Independent work: get the children to collect further examples of irregular verbs from books or other written material.

Plenary: record the children's words and discuss/make observations. There will be patterns (see the chart below). The list is not exhaustive, but a glance through it will sustain the claim that the verbs are to do with everyday life.

LESSON TWO

Introduction: recap on the previous lesson and show the children your enlarged copy of photocopiable page 18. Emphasize the fact that the passage describes everyday life in medieval times. Underline the verbs that are in the past tense. Discuss the kind of verbs they are: *Are the verbs to do with unusual things that the people did or do they describe their everyday lives?*

Using an enlarged copy of photocopiable page 9, set up an ongoing class investigation to which the children can add further examples.

Independent work: when you have an appropriate number of verbs, ask the children to write their own stories about medieval life. They may use photocopiable page 18 as an example. Remind them that, where appropriate, they should use irregular verbs. Refer them to the selection of books on medieval life as a source for reference, as well as the class investigation list.

Plenary: check the collected verbs against the hypothesis that they are to do with everyday life. Sort them into the kinds of categories used in the pie chart. You could display a similar chart in the classroom for the collection of irregular verbs.

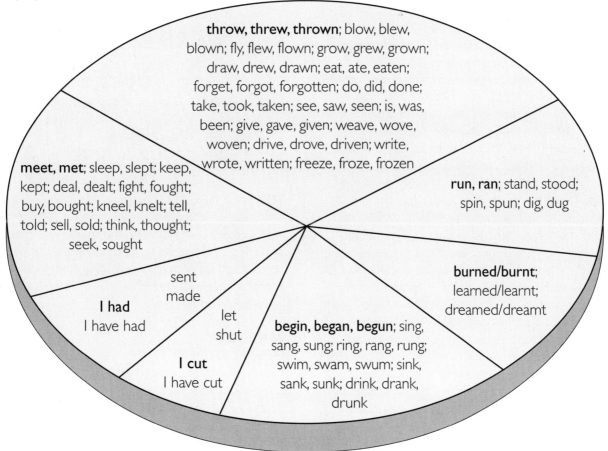

throw, threw, thrown; blow, blew, blown; fly, flew, flown; grow, grew, grown; draw, drew, drawn; eat, ate, eaten; forget, forgot, forgotten; do, did, done; take, took, taken; see, saw, seen; is, was, been; give, gave, given; weave, wove, woven; drive, drove, driven; write, wrote, written; freeze, froze, frozen

meet, met; sleep, slept; keep, kept; deal, dealt; fight, fought; buy, bought; kneel, knelt; tell, told; sell, sold; think, thought; seek, sought

run, ran; stand, stood; spin, spun; dig, dug

sent made

I had
I have had

let
shut

burned/burnt; learned/learnt; dreamed/dreamt

I cut
I have cut

begin, began, begun; sing, sang, sung; ring, rang, rung; swim, swam, swum; sink, sank, sunk; drink, drank, drunk

SPELLING AND GRAMMAR

USING THE APOSTROPHE

LEARNING OBJECTIVE
To learn about the different uses of 's. (Y4/2; P5)

YOU WILL NEED
The coloured poster showing the suffixes that use an apostrophe (the bottom right-hand corner), shared text showing examples of apostrophes, highlighter pens, copies of photocopiable page 19 plus an enlarged copy, writing materials.

WHAT TO DO
The word 'apostrophe' comes from Greek, meaning to turn away. It is used in English to reflect the omission of a letter (or letters) in the written language and sounds in the spoken language, and to mark a relationship between two nouns.

Introduction: Using your shared text, draw attention to the presence of the apostrophe. Highlight each one and the words in which they appear. Explore with the children how some of these words are in fact two words that slide into one. Examine the need for apostrophes in these words: *I'll* and *Ill, We'll* and *Well*. The apostrophe can also be used to indicate a relationship between two adjacent nouns:
The Winter's Tale – a tale told in the winter;
A Midsummer Night's Dream – the kind of dream you might have on a midsummer night;
The Emperor's New Clothes – clothes that belong to the emperor.

The poem on photocopiable page 19 is based upon a poem by Lisel Mueller, 'The Possessive Case' published in 1977 in *The New Yorker*. Use your enlarged copy as a shared text through which to explore relations between adjacent or piggyback nouns using 's. Underline all the instances of 's. Establish that the apostrophe comes between two nouns. Discuss the fact that one noun adds information to another, for example 'mother's blouse'. Take the first noun away and discuss the impact. In this case, we no longer know who owns the blouse. Discuss why it sometimes feels better to use 'of' to join nouns. Explain to the children that where a noun is used to add information about another noun (or piggyback on another noun), we show this by using the suffix 's. As with real piggybacks, you need something to make one part hold on to another. Explain this by saying that this is provided by the 'tongue' of the apostrophe and the 'sticky' of 's'.

Independent work: ask the children to collect more instances of 's and s' using the investigation sheet.

Plenary: explain to the children why we sometimes use 's in preference to s' (we place the apostrophe after the s in nouns that use s to mark the plural).

EXTENSION WORK
Use photocopiable page 19 as a model for producing a class poem.

To introduce the idea of apostrophes joining verbs to nouns or pronouns, use the poster and a shared text, explaining that the apostrophe signals the absence of a letter(s) from the verb and exploring which one(s). The best approach to adopt is that of an ongoing investigation, rather than trying to cover every eventuality in one week. For those children who find it difficult to remember to use it, you can provide an *aide-mémoire* on their writing mats:

> They're not going to Blackpool next week.
> Yes they ARE!

WORD FAMILIES

LEARNING OBJECTIVE
To learn about suffixes that change the part of speech of the word, for example inspector – inspection. (These are shown in the middle of the coloured poster.) (Y5/3; P6)

YOU WILL NEED
The coloured side of the poster, a shared text with examples of words that use suffixes, highlighter pens, paper, felt-tipped pens, Blu-Tack, card arrows to highlight suffixes on the poster, enlarged copies of photocopiable page 9, strips of card with which to make labels for the poster.

WHAT TO DO
Introduction: display the poster and draw attention to the middle of it and the highlighted suffixes. Starting with a word from the shared text, present it along with related words, for example: inspect with inspector and inspection. Work out together what part of speech each of these three words represents.

SPELLING AND GRAMMAR

Independent work: give the children investigation sheets (photocopiable page 9) to investigate other groups of related words and to find out which parts of speech they belong to. This will feed into a class investigation.

Plenary: discuss the children's findings. Agree on the suffixes that are added to make a word into a noun, an adjective, a verb or an adverb. Write a label for the different parts of speech and attach them to the poster with Blu-Tack.

Examine any relevant spelling features at this point using the information in the table below – for instance, nouns ending in 'y' change 'y' to 'i' before adding the suffix: beauty to beautiful, beautician or beautify.

beauty	beautiful (change 'y' to 'i')
happy	happily (change 'y' to 'i')
nature	natural (drop 'e' and add 'al')
artifice	artificial (drop e replace by i and then add al, in order to preserve the soft 'c')
contract	contractual (add 'u' to smooth transition into suffix)
diction	dictionary
adverse	adversary
drama	dramatic
emphasis	emphatic
simple	simplify (drop 'e' as linking vowel is now supplied by the first letter of suffix 'ify')
complex	complicate (follows the same pattern as duplicate, replicate)
drinkable	take off 'able' and you are left with 'drink' (a proper word)
terrible	take off 'ible' and you are left with 'terr' (not a proper word)
invent	inventive (where the word ends in 't', just add 'ive')
sion/tion?	There is a pattern. If the root ends in d, replace by s + ion: cede – cession; lude – lusion; lide – lision; vide – vision. If the root ends in or attracts t, add -ion- invent – inventive – invention; preserve – preservative – preservation
electric	electrician

NB The noun-marking suffix from Latin 'ion' can cause difficulty for children. They tend to write 'conversashun' instead of 'conversation'. Overcome this difficulty by collecting words such as 'opinion, million, Orion' and so on, in which it is very easy to hear the 'ion'. Tell the children that 't' or 's' are responsible for the 'sh' sound

by explaining that these words come to us from Latin via French. The Romans would have said 'teeon'. The French say 'conversaseeyon'. We have simply made it easier by 'modging' (see below) the sound still further to make it sound more 'English', while retaining the Latin spelling. Such words used to be spelled with 'cion' at the end – Chaucer used 'temptacion' – but during the Renaissance (see section 7 of the black and white poster) scholars decided to revert to the Latin spelling with which *they* were more familiar.

Words like 'accommodation', 'suggestion' and so on, where there is a doubling of the consonant, can also cause problems for children. (See pages 7 to 8 for further examples.) Explain that it is a feature of human speech that we make life easy for ourselves. This affects words: 'gotcha' for 'got you', 'could of' for 'could have' and 'gonna' for 'going to'. This process is called assimilation or 'modging'. The Romans were good at modging. Instead of 'conlapse', they said 'collapse'; instead of 'inpossible', they said 'impossible'; instead of 'inlusive', they said 'illusive'. The assimilation process is reflected in the spelling with a doubling of the initial letter of the root word to indicate the absent letter. Shakespeare made up the word 'adconmodation' which he, being aware of the modging effect, wrote down as 'accommodation'.

Liven up this 'modging' story by telling the children that two Roman soldiers were eating their sandwiches one day on Hadrian's wall, when one of them 'modged' with his mouth full:
'Do you think the Picts could climb this wall?'
'Impossible!' said his friend, with his mouth full of goat butty.
'What did you say? IMpossible. That sounds easier to say than INpossible. Great word – I think we should tell the others.'

PREFIXES AND ROOTS

LEARNING OBJECTIVE
To explore how to build words from a root and an affix. (Y5/3; P6)

YOU WILL NEED
The House at Pooh Corner by A.A. Milne (Methuen), shared text showing examples of root words and prefixes (see photocopiable pages 21 and 22 for lists of possible roots and prefixes), the coloured side of the poster, enlarged copy of photocopiable page 20, copies of photocopiable page 20 for each child, highlighter pens, adult dictionaries.

SPELLING AND GRAMMAR

WHAT TO DO

Introduction: a good introductory text for this activity is the 'Contradiction' in A.A. Milne's *The House at Pooh Corner*, in which the characters speculate on the meaning of 'introduction' and 'contradiction' and whether they are opposites. The passage uses the prefixes 'intro-' and 'contra-' with the roots '-dict/duct'.

Display enlarged versions of photocopiable pages 21 and 22 and discuss the full list of prefixes and suffixes with the class. Highlight a word from the shared text that contains a prefix. Ask the children to find the prefix on the poster. Discuss another word that uses the same prefix but has a different root.

Now, using your enlarged copy of photocopiable page 20, enter the root into the central box of the top half and the prefix into the central box of the bottom half.

Enter workable prefixes in the four boxes of the top box and workable roots in the four boxes of the bottom box as shown. Show the children how to word build, check and add to their words using the dictionary. Show them how to use the spaces by the dots to record the words they have found.

Independent work: give each child a copy of photocopiable page 20. Point out to the children that they do not need to fill in all the spaces. Using their sheets, half the class should investigate the meaning of a root chosen by you and/or the children, and the other half the meaning of the prefix chosen by you and/or the children in the same way as outlined above.

Plenary: take feedback from the children and establish the meaning of the root and prefix.

Extension work: sort the prefixes into those that: help words say the opposite; show position; show direction; show time and order; show number, quantity or size.

con		ex
◆ contract		◆ extract
◆ contractor		◆ extraction
◆ contractile	tract	◆ extractor
◆		◆ extractable

re		de
◆ retract		◆ detract
◆ retractible		◆ detractor
◆ retraction		◆ detractive
◆		◆

Meaning of root:

mit		pose
◆ submit		◆ suppose
◆ submissive		◆ supposition
◆ submission	sub	◆
◆		◆
◆		◆ success
◆ subvert		◆ succeed
◆ subversive		◆ succession

vert		ceed

Meaning of prefix:

COMPOUND WORDS

LEARNING OBJECTIVE
To understand that whole words can be put together to make new words. (Y3/2; P4)

YOU WILL NEED
Shared text including compound words, photocopiable page 23, picture of the car below drawn on to a board or flip chart or reproduced on an OHT.

WHAT TO DO
Introduction: introduce compound words by explaining that, like German (refer to section 3 of the black and white poster) new words can be made in English by putting words together: Armbanduhr = arm band clock = wristwatch; Kuhlschrank = cool cupboard = fridge; Staubsauger = dustsucker = vacuum cleaner. Look at the compound words on the car picture. Introduce the term 'compound'. Look at the shared text for further examples.

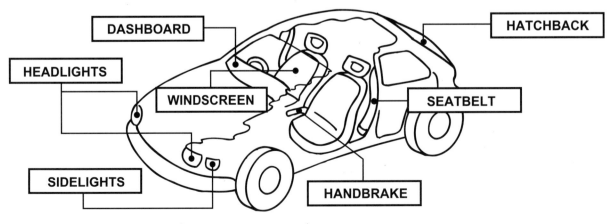

DASHBOARD HATCHBACK HEADLIGHTS WINDSCREEN SEATBELT SIDELIGHTS HANDBRAKE

SPELLING AND GRAMMAR

Compound words have come into the language because the existing stock of words has often been unable to respond to the demands being put upon it through new inventions or situations. Explore this with the children by taking a topic, such as space travel, and investigating how many new compound words have come into the language as a result of this – liftoff, spacewalk, spacesuit, spacecraft, spacewoman/man – are just some examples.

Independent work: groups of children can collect compound words, write the constituents on separate pieces of card and then present them to another group to reassemble. Another group can have a go at collecting and presenting a different set of compound words. They will soon have enough cards to play 'Compound word snap' or 'Pairs' ('Pelmanism').

Get the children to choose words and make up compound equivalents, for example: 'daffodil' becomes 'trumpetflower', 'soap' becomes 'bubblecake', 'road' becomes 'motorsnake' and 'river' becomes 'waterribbon'. Again, this activity could be extended to become a matching game between word and compound version. It could also be a good springboard into poetry.

Use photocopiable page 23 as a model. The words are loosely linked around themes. You could use this as a model for individual composition in shared writing with children or use it to support teaching the concept of compound words.

HOMOPHONES

LEARNING OBJECTIVE
To understand that not all words that sound the same are spelled the same. (Y3/3; P4)

YOU WILL NEED
A shared text containing homophones, paper, felt-tipped pens.

WHAT TO DO
Introduction: homophones (words that sound alike, but vary in spelling, such as 'here' and 'hear') can be a source of difficulty for children. They need to understand the context in which the homophone occurs, as well as being able to remember how to spell it.

Introduce some exemplar homophones. (You may like to use the ones shown in the illustration.) Elicit from the children the observation that the words sound the same but look different. Introduce the term 'homophone'. Make the connection with telephone, microphone and xylophone in which 'phone' carries the meaning 'sound'. Repeat the term as you collect further examples.

Looking at the context in which the words are used, and making up a sentence with them in as an *aide-mémoire* for their writing mat is a useful approach. The children may also find it helpful if you offer them the explanations given below to help them differentiate.

two	relate to words in which you can hear the 'w' – twelve, twenty, between, twin
there	relate to where and here
would	relate to could and should
pear	remember this by saying 'The bear with a pear'
reign	relate to regal in which you can hear the 'g' from Latin 'regere' to rule (see section 3 of the black and white poster on Latin Influence)
eight	relate this to the German 'acht' from which this word is derived (see section 3 of the black and white poster)
pale	relate to 'pallid' Latin for 'pale'
knight	relate to OE 'cniht' meaning 'servant' (see section 4 of the black and white poster)
knot	relate to OE 'cnotta'
sum	relate to Latin 'summa' meaning 'the top' giving 'sum' and 'summit'
write	relate to OE 'writan' meaning 'to scratch runes into bark'
threw	relate to blew, the 'ew' representing the irregular past tense
see	point out that you have two eyes, and there are two 'e's in the word

Independent work: ask the children to write sentences in which they deliberately write in the wrong word. They then exchange these with other children who should write in the correct version.

Plenary: ask the children to justify the corrections they have made to each other's work.

SPELLING AND GRAMMAR

Name _____   Date _____

Everyday life in the olden days

The men drove cattle and sheep to market where they sold them.

The women wove baskets and spun wool.

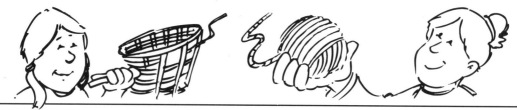

They grew vegetables and caught fish.

In the autumn they went to the fair.
They drank ale and ate salted pork in the winter.

They told stories round the fire and sang songs.

At Christmas the church bells rang.

SPELLING AND GRAMMAR

Name ——————————————   Date ——————————————

Piggyback poem

My mother's blouse
My brother's louse.
   Le train de grande vitesse
   L'auberge de jeunesse
     The hostess trolley.
       Aladdin's cave
       Santa's grotto
       Our Maddy's Dave
       The Girl Guide motto.
The Flight of the Bumblebee
The kipper's whiskers.
The Battle of Britain
The cat's knickers.
      Little Red Riding Hood's New Clothes
      The Emperor's Grandma.
  A piece of cake
  A piece of my mind.
  Peace of mind.
     My mother's house
     My brother's mouse.

PHOTOCOPIABLE
RESOURCE
BANK

SPELLING AND GRAMMAR

Name _____   Date _____

Prefixes and roots

◆
◆
◆
◆

◆
◆
◆
◆

◆
◆
◆
◆

◆
◆
◆
◆

Meaning of root:

◆
◆
◆
◆
◆
◆
◆
◆

◆
◆
◆
◆
◆
◆
◆
◆

Meaning of prefix:

SPELLING AND GRAMMAR

Name —————————————— Date ——————————————

Roots

This is a list of some roots. A good dictionary will give their meanings. Remember that roots can change – for example, 'cede' can become 'cession'.

C	D	F	G	H	J	L
-cede	-dict-	-fact-	-gest-	-here-	-ject-	-lapse
-clude	-doct-	-fect-	-gress-	-hes-		-lat-
-clus	-duct-	-fend-		-hibit		-lect-
-curs		-fens-				-lide
-cuss		-fer-				-locate
		-fid				-loqu-
		-fin-				-lude
		-flect-				-lus-
		-flict-				
		-flu-				
		-form-				

M	N	P	R	S	T	V
-mand-	-nounce	-pel-	-rogat-	-scribe-	-tact-	-vad
	(nunc)	-pul		-scrip		-vas
-mit-		-pend-	-rect-	-secut-	-tect-	-vent-
-mot-		-port-	-rupt-	-serv-	-tain-	-vers-
		-pose		-sess-	-tract-	-vict-
		-poss-		-sist-		-vide-
		-press-		-solut-		-viv
				-spir-		-volent
				-spect		-volut-
				-stant		
				-stinct		
				-sume		

PHOTOCOPIABLE
RESOURCE
BANK

Name —————————————— Date ——————————————

Prefixes and their meanings

Old English	
	a – on, in, towards, in the state of
	be – cover/affect completely/cause to be/cover with
	for– indicating rejection/prohibition/intensity
	fore – before/earlier
	mis – wrong/bad
	over – excessive/superior/location/movement above and down
	un – not/contrary to
	under – below/underneath/of lesser importance
	with – against/away

Latin		
	ab – away	ad – to/towards
	ante – before	bene – well
	bi – two	circum – around
	con – with, together	contra – against
	de – down	dis – lack of, removal, reversal
	ex – out of	extra – outside, beyond
	in – in, into	inter – between
	intra – within, side	male – bad
	multi – many	non – negation
	ob – towards, away from	per – through
	post – after	pre – before
	pro – in favour of, supporting, forward	re – again
	sub – under	super – above, outstanding, greater size
	trans – across	
	tri – three	uni – one

Greek		
	a – not	anti – against
	auto – self	dia – through
	epi – upon, above, in addition	hyper – too much
	hypo – beneath	macro – large, long, great in size
	micro – small	
	poly – much many	peri – round
	tele – from a distance	syn – with or together

PHOTOCOPIABLE
RESOURCE BANK

SPELLING AND GRAMMAR

Name _____   Date _____

Compound words

Playgroup
Playground
Roundabout
Lost and found.

Seesaw
Sycamore
Gewgaw
Jackdaw.

Dewson
Jenkinson
Bricklayer
Soothsayer
Hebblethwaite
Paperweight.

Waylay
Moonday
Moonshine
Sunshine
Sunday
Day's eye
Daisy
Easy-peasy.

Peanuts
Peasouper
Fogbound
Safe and sound.

Underground
Seedbed
Dandelion
Weedbed.

Bedrock
Rockfish
Fishfinger
Humdinger
Hummingbird
Cowherd.

Coxswain
Bosun
Porthole
Portcullis
Snaggletooth
Sourpuss
Smoothtongue
Sugarplum.

HISTORY AND INFLUENCES

This section deals with the major factors responsible for the maze that constitutes our spelling system, namely the multitude of sources for the vocabulary of English. It looks at how the spelling of imported words tends to be left untouched, and explores the influences behind the evolution of the spelling system. When the layers of often conflicting spelling systems are unravelled, it is possible to see patterns and regularities that are directly attributable to the origin of the words under investigation. By the same token, it is possible to explain the seemingly unfathomable by recourse to the people and events in history that directly influenced spelling.

The black and white side of the poster, which documents the milestones in the development of the language, will be useful in supporting the children's investigations. This section of the book highlights areas of interest to investigate, and provides explanations which can be brought to life through the black and white poster. Teaching spelling does not take the path of the evolution of spelling as shown on the poster. Therefore, in your detailed use of the black and white poster you may find that you 'jump around'. You will need to teach to the children's needs – not to history! (Again, the activities in this section are ordered as they occur in the NLS *Framework*.)

THE HISTORY BEHIND THE LETTERS AND LETTER STRINGS

The information that follows will also help you to support children in their exploration of the occurrence of certain letters/letter strings, and in deducing some of the conventions for using them at the beginning, in the middle and at the end of words – also see photocopiable pages 7 and 8. (This is specifically a Y4 requirement in the NLS *Framework*.)

The alphabet is our resource for recording spoken sounds. The way in which this resource is used has evolved over the centuries and is closely bound up with the history of English. When children know that there are patterns in the use of the letters and have a rough idea of their regularity, they will have greater confidence in making a correct guess when spelling an unknown word, and they will have greater success in learning the patterns if they understand their nature and origin.

Different languages favour different letters for representing speech sounds. For example, many 'sk' words came from Norse, while 'sc' is generally used in French or Greek words. As a general guideline, 'sc' is used before consonants (for example, script) and before certain vowels (scant, scour). Although it does come before 'e' and 'i', it does not retain its hard sound. The letters 'sk' are used before 'e' and 'i' – skew, skim – where the presence of 'k' helps to preserve the hard sound. Both 'scu' and 'sku' occur. Children can investigate the use of 'sc' and 'sk', firstly as a whole-class activity and then in group work. You may like to ask them to make a bar graph of the number of words that use 'sc' and 'sk'. They could then investigate further by looking more closely – 'sca'/'ska', 'sco'/'sko', 'scu'/'sku'. They could also examine the derivation of the words that use 'sc' and 'sk'.

The letters 'k' and 'c' can both be used to represent the hard 'k' sound. Again there are patterns to their use. For example, 'ka' words are far less frequent than 'ca' words and words that use 'ka' tend to be more unusual. There are far more 'cl'/'cr' words than 'kl'/'kr' words. Notwithstanding the fact that 'c' combines with 'e', 'i', 'y' and 'h', which lengthens the dictionary entry, the letter 'c' is used far more frequently. Overall, the 'k' words are generally more unusual.

HISTORY AND INFLUENCES

Before the Norman conquest, the Roman alphabet was used to write down Old English. The letters 'j' and 'w' were not in the alphabet and 'qu' and 'z' were avoided. When the Normans came (see section 5 of the black and white poster), the scribes did not care for Old English 'cw' and changed it to 'qu' as a result of Latin influence on French – quando (L) and quand (F). You may like to ask children to select 'qu' words from their dictionary and to investigate their origin.

The Romans used the letter 'i' in words that now have a 'j' – iustitia for justice. 'J' is often followed by 'a', 'o' and 'u'. Again, children could investigate the frequency of 'ge' and 'gi' (making the soft sound) as opposed to 'je' and 'ji' and compare the origins of words that attract the 'ge' spelling as opposed to 'je'.

The Romans used the letter 'v' for the 'w' sound. Many words beginning with 'w' are Old English in derivation. In this respect, you will not find many 'wu' words as the Norman scribes did not like the combination of 'wu' or 'triple u' (see section 5 of the black and white poster). Many words that sound as though they should have 'wu' at the beginning have 'wa' or 'wo'. The Norman scribes also did not like u and m, n or v as these combinations were hard to read in their handwriting. For this reason, they changed the vowel to 'o' as in money, love and so on (investigate this using photocopiable page 31).

A brief glance at the dictionary entry for 'z' reveals a welter of unusual words. Ask children to list words that begin with the letter 'z'. There won't be many. Looking at the language of origin of these words is particularly interesting. The first four in the Collins *Shorter English Dictionary* come from Italian, Japanese and Russian.

The letters 'oi' often denote that the word is of French origin. Again, you could set up a class investigation of this by finding words with 'oi' in and checking their origin in the dictionary. The letters 'oi' generally occur in the middle or at the beginning of words. You could also investigate words such as royal, oyster and doyen, which have all passed through French on their way into English.

The letters 'gh' were introduced by the Dutch printers who came over to England with William Caxton in 1476 (see section 6 of the black and white poster). The combination of 'gh' is one favoured by the Dutch, as in Vincent van Gogh, for example. These letters infiltrated our spelling system at the beginning of words, in the middle and at the end. For example, 'gost', 'gastly' and 'gerkin' acquired 'gh' at this time. Words in Old English with an 'h' representing 'ch' as in 'loch', acquired the 'gh' so 'niht' changed to 'night'. (This also happened to some French words by analogy – delight, haughty, spright. They should not have acquired it as 'delight' is related to 'delicious', 'haughty' to 'haut(e)' as in 'haute couture' and 'hauteur', see clothes labels, and 'sprightly' to 'sprite'). Again, Old English words with 'h' at the end acquired 'gh' in the name of aesthetics. (see section 6 of the black and white poster). It could also have been for ease as 'g' would have been stored next to 'h' in the case of letters! Once again, when children know this, they are better able to remember the patterns.

HISTORY AND INFLUENCES

These activities are designed for whole class and group work, starting with a shared text as a springboard in many instances. The introduction is intended to take about five minutes, with investigation work taking roughly 20 minutes (it may take several sessions so you may need to allow a 'real-time' investigation for as long as it takes) and the plenary ten minutes. The NLS *Framework* Year and Term references are given in brackets at the end of the learning objectives.

HOW 'EL' BECAME 'LE'

LEARNING OBJECTIVES
To investigate the spelling pattern 'le' and understand how it came to be. To understand where 'le' occurs in order to differentiate the different spellings of words ending with the phoneme /əl/. (Y3/2; P4)

YOU WILL NEED
The black and white poster (section 5), shared text showing words ending in 'le', photocopiable page 9, blank cards.

WHAT TO DO
Introduction: Using the shared text, draw attention to words ending in 'le'. Discuss common spelling problems with this ending. Children will, for instance, suggest 'ul', 'al' and 'el' or 'ol' for this sound (and possibly others).
Independent work: Now set up an investigation into the various possibilities discussed as well as 'le'. (The purpose of this is to establish that the usual way of representing the sound is with the letters 'al' or 'le', although 'el' will also be found in words like 'chapel', 'libel', and so on.)
Plenary: Draw attention to the possibilities that have been uncovered by the investigation. Go back to your original list and put question marks next to 'ul' and any other unlikely versions. Be careful not to reject them entirely because you may find names of commercial products with 'odd' spellings, such as 'Dettol'.

Discuss the findings: *So, we have apple, bottle, cable and castle. What kind of words are these? Are they nouns or adjectives?* Repeat with words such as natural, magical, responsible, drinkable, and so on. If necessary, use a separate category for nouns ending in 'el'. Set up the hypothesis that nouns end in 'le'/'el', whereas adjectives end in 'al', 'ible'/'able'.

EXTENSION WORK
As a further investigation, using photocopiable page 9, ask the children to sort the words into 'le'/'el' nouns and 'al', 'ible'/'able' adjectives (you may like to do this in the second 20 minutes, if you are using the Literacy Hour lesson structure), and ask them to check out the hypothesis that nouns end in 'le'/'el' whereas adjectives end in 'al' 'ible'/'able'.

In the plenary session, look at findings and decide whether the hypothesis was correct. Are there any exceptions? (for example, 'sandal'.)

Refer to the black and white poster. Explain that originally Old English words ended in 'el'/'ol' – aeppel, cradol – but the French monks who had the task of writing English down preferred to see 'le' at the ends of words because this reflected the spelling in their language – bataille = battle, bouteille = bottle. This pattern came to be transferred to many Old English and Latin words, for example buckle (buccula), bugle (bugula) and castellum (castle).

Children can go on to make a poster of nouns that end in 'le'. They could also show the language of origin and the original word, alongside the modern version.

Get children to examine commercial labelling and to collect unusual ways of writing the sound represented by the letters 'le', for instance Panadol.

Continue the investigation into adjectives ending in 'al', 'ible'/'able'. Children could prepare pairs of cards for matching as shown below.

architecture	architectural

Draw out the pattern in the use of 'ible'/'able': *What do you notice about presentable, drinkable, responsible? Can you see any whole words inside the longer words? Is there a pattern?* Make sure that the children know that these can be tricky words that they may have to learn to check in a dictionary.

THE MYSTERY OF THE SILENT LETTER

LEARNING OBJECTIVE
To become aware of the occurrence of silent letters. (Y3/2; P4)

YOU WILL NEED
Enlarged copies of photocopiable page 32, shared text showing examples of words with silent letters, large sheet of paper, paper, felt-tipped pens.

WHAT TO DO

Introduction and independent work: use the shared text to initiate a brainstorm of words that have silent letters in them. Start a class collection on a large sheet of paper. When you have a large enough collection, start to investigate them.

Words with silent letters can be divided into two groups. There are words with silent letters in (either in the middle or at the end) that are related to words in which you can hear the silent letter. The words below can be recorded on photocopiable page 32: bomb/bombard, climb/clamp and clamber, thumb/thimble, crumb/crumble, dumb/stumble (to do with the inability to speak and stammering), solemn/solemnity, condemn/condemnation, plumber/plumbago, sign/signal, reign/regal, doubt/dubious, debt/debit, receipt/reception, broad/breadth, long/length, wide/width, soft/soften, strong/strength.

Other words have come from Germanic/Latin/Greek sources and retain traces of their original spelling, even though the pronunciation has changed, for example:
◆ pt/ps from Greek as in pterodactyl and psychology;
◆ kn from Old English/German where the 'k' would originally have been pronounced;
◆ night etc. was originally 'niht' but was changed to 'gh' to represent the 'ch' sound as in 'loch';
◆ wr as in wrist is Old English/German;
◆ wh was originally 'hw' to reflect the breathy pronunciation (see the pronunciation of 'who').

Use the black and white poster to explore these words and how they entered the language.

Demonstrate the shift in the pronunciation of words by playing Chinese Whispers with a single nonsense word. This will mirror the evolution of pronunciation over time and will enable children to understand the spelling system more clearly.

VOWELS AT THE END OF WORDS

LEARNING OBJECTIVE
To be aware of the effect of the 'magic e'.
(Y5/1; P6)

YOU WILL NEED
The black and white side of the poster (sections 7 and 8), shared text showing words that end in a variety of vowels, world map, photocopiable page 9, food labels (especially those from other countries), dictionaries that show the origins of words, a residential telephone directory.

WHAT TO DO
Introduction: using the shared text, draw attention to words that end in a variety of vowels, including words that have a long vowel ending in 'e' such as 'cake'.

With reference to the poster, explain that Richard Mulcaster was the 'inventor' of 'e' at the end of words which had a long vowel in them. He wanted to show in the way the words are written that the vowel is longer. Compare words like 'run' and 'rune'. Likewise, he did not like to see words ending in 'v' or 's' making a 'z' sound. He 'tidied' these up by deciding that they too should end in 'e'.

Make a list of 've' words. (There are at least two exceptions that do not use 've' – spiv and Slav). They are all examples of how context – position within a word – and the surrounding sounds can influence spelling. Turning to the words that end in vowels other than 'e', make a list of them from the shared text.

Now use the food labels to demonstrate how words ending in vowels other than 'e' are likely to be words from other languages. For example, 'pizza' and 'spaghetti' are from Italy, 'muesli' from Switzerland, 'tuna' from Greek via Spanish and 'fetta' from Greek. Another good source of words for this exercise is from car advertisements – Sierra, Fiesta, Seicento; the telephone directory can also be very useful for observing the spelling of different surnames. Speculate with the children as to which language the words in the shared text might come from and get them to check in a dictionary. Enter the words on the world map. (You may like to have this permanently on display or simply get it out when appropriate. It provides a useful and effective way of collecting words.) Consider the reason why the word might have entered the language – perhaps it is a legacy of the Empire, from the

HISTORY AND INFLUENCES

Norman conquest, from travel around Europe or other continents, from groups of people coming to live in this country, politics, geography, the arts, food, and so on. Refer to section 8 of the black and white poster.

Independent work: children can play the following game, using the words in the list below and dictionaries that show word origins. (Note that the words do not necessarily end in a vowel.) Provide a list of six words (see the list for suggestions and origins). Tell the children to find out which language the words come from and their meanings. They should write down their definitions by the side of the words, making sure that at least two are false definitions.

Plenary: in the plenary, ask the children to present their words to the class. Get the rest of the class to vote as to which definitions are false. Enter the words on the world map and discuss with the children how they may have entered the English language.

EXTENSION WORK

Investigate how these words are made into plurals – pianos and tomatoes. (See 'Suffixes for plurality' on page 10). Names of artists/countries also provide a useful springboard for discussing unusual letter strings – van Gogh, Rousseau, Gauguin, Monet, Venezuela, Ecuador, and so on.

DOUBLING CONSONANTS

LEARNING OBJECTIVE
To know when to double letters, for example before adding -ing. (Y5/1; P6)

YOU WILL NEED
The black and white side of the poster (section 7), photocopiable page 9 enlarged to A3, a shared text.

INUIT	anorak, kayak
AMERINDIAN	chili, chocolate, cocoa, potato, tapioca, tobacco, tomato, toucan, maize
CARIBBEAN	calypso, canoe, limbo, reggae
FINNISH	sauna
MAGYAR	paprika, goulash, coach
WEST AND CENTRAL AFRICAN	banana, chimpanzee, baobab
RUSSIAN	tsar, bolshevik, perestroika, glasnost, steppe
SCANDINAVIAN	fjord, LEGO, saga, ransack, sky, skin, kettle, skirt, wrong
TURKISH	kaftan, yoghurt, tulip
HEBREW	abacus, amen, alleluia, cinnamon,
SWAHILI	safari
ITALIAN	soprano, alto, concert, cello, violin, piano, forte, crescendo, aria
GREEK	rhythm, melody, symphony, polygon, rhombus, diagonal, parallelogram, trapezium, dodecahedron, cathedral, mystery, rhetoric, synagogue, apostle, pope, dolphin, kaleidoscope, galaxy, elastic
ARABIC	apricot, carob, cotton, genie, giraffe, jar, jumper, lemon, minaret, mosque, saracen, sherbet, sultana, sorbet, zenith, zero
JAPANESE	bonsai, karate, kimono, satsuma, Toyota, futon, karaoke
POLYNESIAN	tattoo, ukelele
AUSTRALIAN ABORIGINE	boomerang, budgerigar, kangaroo, koala
SANSKRIT/HINDI	bangle, bungalow, calico, chutney, curry, gymkhana, juggernaut, khaki, pagoda, polo, pyjamas, shampoo, thug, yoga
PERSIAN	caravan, jasmine, orange, pagoda, turban
CHINA	china, chop-chop, cumquat, kaolin, kung fu, lychee, ping pong, shantung, tea, typhoon, yen
MALAY	bamboo, cockatoo, compound, orangutang, rattan, sago, teak
FRENCH	buffet, valet, maisonette, cordon bleu, hotel, restaurant
DUTCH	knapsack, sketch, hobble, yacht, trek
GERMAN	rucksack, spire, yodel, hamburger, lager

HISTORY AND INFLUENCES

WHAT TO DO

Double consonants occur in the middle of words, for example rabble, pebble, nibble, hobble and stubble, in order to preserve the short vowel (compare to cable, bible). They also appear in words like stop/stopped/stopping, again to preserve the short vowel (compare hope/hoping, hop/hopping). Richard Mulcaster (see section 7 of the poster), a Renaissance scholar, wrote the *Elementarie* in 1582. This book was his attempt to reform the spelling system. In it he proposed that double consonants should serve a purpose and that they should occur where one syllable ends and another begins. Over time this came to be applied to words with short vowels.

Introduction and independent work: using the poster, introduce the character of Richard Mulcaster and set up photocopiable page 9 as shown. Use a shared text as the stimulus.

NB The letters 'ff', 'll', 'ss' and 'zz' appear after short vowels at the end of words. Children may notice this and wish to discuss it. Strictly speaking, the investigation should focus on common two syllable

bb	bubble
dd	muddle
ff	sniffy
gg	bigger
hh	??
jj	??
kk	??

words such as those shown and those with the suffixes 'ing', 'er' and 'ed'. Children may come up with words like 'success' and 'commit'. If they do, put them into a separate category and consider the explanation given on page 15. Use photocopiable pages 7 and 8 (consonant profiles).

Notice that consonants that never or only rarely double (such as trekking) have been deliberately included to stimulate discussion: *Why doesn't 'h' double? How often does it come at the end of words? What job does it do?* (Discussion can follow about how 'h' combines with 'c', 's' and 't' to make new sounds). *Is 'j' used in the middle or end of words? What is used instead? Why don't we double 'v' or 'w'? What would they look like? What sounds do the letters 'cc' represent in words like 'success'? What letters do you need to use if you just want /k/ (for example, 'ck' in 'buckle')?* (Note that 'soccer' is an exception. It comes from 'Association football' where, interestingly enough, the 'c' is soft.)

Plenary: when the investigation is complete, with up to five entries next to each double consonant (where possible), discuss the findings. Draw attention to the fact that the consonant doubles in order to preserve the short vowel, particularly when the word ends in 'le' or the suffixes 'ed', 'er', 'est' and 'ing'.

EXTENSION WORK

In a shared writing lesson, make up a poem using double consonant words. For example:

SHOPPING
Trolleys clattering
Nerves shattering
Children chattering.
Carriers popping
Bottles dropping
I hate shopping.
Assistants muttering
Spreads buttering
Credit cards fluttering.

SCHWIBBLY SCHWA

LEARNING OBJECTIVE
To understand about and be able to identify words that have an unstressed vowel. To explore ways of remembering to spell them correctly.
(Y5/3; P6)

YOU WILL NEED
Writing materials, paper, felt-tipped pens.

WHAT TO DO
Introduction: children often have difficulty with polysyllabic words. Such words often have an unstressed vowel. This tends to have an indeterminate quality and its phonetic label is 'schwa'.

Start to explore this with children by taking the word 'company' as a starting point. Break it into syllables – com – pa – ny, but do not write it down at this point. Make sure you say it in natural way, without stressing the second syllable. Draw a box with three compartments as shown below.

HISTORY AND INFLUENCES

With the children, work through the syllables, assigning letters to the sound as you go. If the children know how to spell the word, steer the discussion to cover the fact that the 'a' in the second syllable does not sound like an 'a'. Alternatively, if the children have difficulty in spelling this word they may make all kinds of suggestions for the letter to represent this sound. Either way, you will have a discussion point: *Sometimes we write sounds in an unusual way and this can cause problems for us.*

Discuss the sound of the endings of the words, the fact that the sound is the same each time, but that there are different ways of writing it. Introduce the term 'schwibbly schwa'.

Independent work: organize the children into pairs and ask them to spell the following words: possib**le**, gentl**e**men, wom**a**n, **o**blige, s**u**ppose, p**a**rticul**a**r, teach**e**r, doct**o**r, fam**ou**s, col**ou**r, fig**u**re, fib**re**. (The unstressed vowel is shown in bold, but do not stress it as you say the words.)

Plenary: discuss the findings – the sound is the same each time but can be represented in different ways. It attracts almost every vowel letter and combinations of vowel letters with the letter 'r'. Flag this up as a source of difficulty and suggest that the children always check 'schwibbly schwa' – the sound you can't get hold of – in a dictionary if they are not sure.

Refer to the history of the language and the influence of German, Latin and Greek offering this as an explanation for the apparent 'chaos'. This is part of the problem – and the solution – when it comes to remembering which spelling to use. The children may find it helpful if you give them the following:

tink**er** from Kestelflick**er** (German)
tail**or** from rabberciat**ore** or sail**or** from navigat**ore** (Italian)

Here are some more ways that might also help the children to remember how to write these unstressed syllables. Introduce them as needs arise:

company, oblige	relate to companion/obligatory, in which you can hear the vowel
possible	relate to suffix 'ible' (see page 26)
gentlemen	discuss the constituents of this compound word – gentle, men
suppose	relate to the prefix sub- (see pages 15–16)
particular	relate to solar, lunar, similar, polar etc and 'word within a word'
teacher	relate to the suffix 'er' used with verbs to convert them into nouns (see page 14)
doctor	relate to words like actor, sector, conductor, tractor and so on
famous	relate to similar words – curious, furious, hideous, treacherous. (Note that it is an ending for adjectives.)
colour	relate to honour, valour, glamour
figure	relate to nature, architecture and figurative, natural
fibre	many of these 're' words are Greek. The 're' structure is echoed in related words, such as 'theatre' and 'theatrical', 'centre' and 'central'

Name ——————————————————— Date ———————————————

The history of English: the Norman monks

Collect words that the Norman monks changed because they were hard to read in their writing.

Here is one to start you off:

OLD WAY

luv

NEW WAY

love

Name ———————————————   Date ———————————————

Silent (?) letters

plumber

plumbago

PHOTOCOPIABLE
RESOURCE
BANK